At the limit of breath

THE UNIVERSITY OF ALBERTA PRESS

Poems on the films of Jean-Luc Godard

t the limit of breath

Stephen Scobie

Published by

The University of Alberta Press
Ring House 2
Edmonton, Alberta, Canada T6G 2E1
www.uap.ualberta.ca

Copyright © 2013 Stephen Scobie

LIBRARY AND ARCHIVES CANADA CATALOGUING IN PUBLICATION

Scobie, Stephen, 1943–, author
    At the limit of breath : poems on the films of Jean-Luc Godard / Stephen Scobie.

(Robert Kroetsch series)
Issued in print and electronic formats.
ISBN 978-0-88864-671-2 (pbk.).—ISBN 978-0-88864-742-9 (pdf).—ISBN 978-0-88864-740-5 (epub).—
ISBN 978-0-88864-741-2 (Amazon kindle)

    1. Godard, Jean Luc, 1930– —Poetry. 2. Motion pictures—Poetry. I. Title.
II. Series: Robert Kroetsch series

PS8587.C6A86 2013   C811'.54   C2013-904964-9
                                 C2013-904965-7

First edition, first printing, 2013.
Printed and bound in Canada by Houghton Boston Printers, Saskatoon Saskatchewan.
Copyediting and Proofreading by Peter Midgley.

A volume in the Robert Kroetsch series.

The University of Alberta Press is committed to protecting our natural environment. As part of our efforts,
this book is printed on Enviro Paper: it contains 100% post-consumer recycled fibres and is acid- and
chlorine-free.

The University of Alberta Press gratefully acknowledges the support received for its publishing program
from The Canada Council for the Arts. The University of Alberta Press also gratefully acknowledges the
financial support of the Government of Canada through the Canada Book Fund (CBF) and the Government
of Alberta through the Alberta Multimedia Development Fund (AMDF) for its publishing activities.

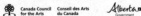

People in love
quote as they please

so we have the right
to quote as we please. Therefore,

I show people quoting,
merely making sure

that they quote what pleases me.

— JLG, 1962

Whatever has been well said by anyone
is mine.

— *Seneca, 1st century A D*

An image is the pure
creation of the soul. It is born

not simply by comparison, but by
the coming together of two

more or less distant realities. The more
the connections between these realities

are true and distant,
distant and true,

the more the image will move you,
the more it will be

pure poetry. What is great
is not the image, but

the emotion the image evokes.
If this image is true, distant and true,

then you are given
the measure of the emotion,

the image of the measure.

> — *adapted from*
> *Pierre Reverdy*, Nord-Sud, *1918.*

Here is light
and here are soldiers

here are bosses
here are children

here is light
and here is joy

here is war
here is the angel

and here is fear
and here is light

here is the universal wound
here is night

here is the virgin
here is grace

and here is light
and here is light

and here is fog
and here is adventure

and here is fiction
and here is reality

and here is documentary
and here is movement

and here is cinema
and here is the image

and here is sound
and here is cinema

here is cinema
here is cinema

There is work

— JLG, Scénario du film Passion, 1982

Contents

À bout de souffle Breathless

At the edge, at the limit of breath,
time for a new sensation —
the gun abrupt and clumsy in his hands.

Thumb tracing the line of his lip,
sun-dazzle over trees, and then the bridge,
the river flowing under Notre-Dame.

Her T-shirt on the Avenue, tribune:
herald of a new wave rising.
Tonight I will be with you in Paradise.

What you believe in the long conversation,
Matisse and Renoir on the wall, the tiny room
filled by a bed and William Faulkner.

The man on the street pointing him out, and
pointing you the way to go. A phone call's betrayal —
dégueulasse.

Trying to reach the intersection,
rue Campagne-Première:
staggering, falling, falling again.

What does it mean?
What does that strange word mean?

Le petit soldat The Little Soldier

1960

Not a general, not a commander:
just a small soldier
in a small and dirty war.

So, not a spectacular torture: nothing
to leave any mark: wet cloth
smothering the face, the limit of breath,

monotonous and sad. At worst,
electrodes to the toes. It doesn't matter
which side are you on.

By the waters of Leman I sat down and wept

and across its bridges, back and forth
past Rousseau's island
in a big American car.

I'm listening to the universe

and watching her Danish hair
as it sways before the camera lens
interrogation. What are you thinking, what

is anyone thinking?
Il faut savoir. A photograph
is truth, and cinema is truth

24 times per second. Lie to me.

Nothing but guns and cigarettes
until she disappears, abruptly, off-screen,
and the whole film

runs like crazy to its ending.
"One thing I've learned is not to be bitter,"
he tells us, bitterly.

Une femme est une femme
A Woman is a Woman
1961

Lights, camera, action! — all the exciting toys, wide-screen
and Eastmancolor, stretching the line into Cinemascope, as wide, as wide,

as wide as it will go. And as for Karina —

she's not just walking the streets of Saint-Denis, she's dancing them —
and little old ladies had better step aside, there goes Raoul

and this time he's got the anamorphic lens, there's space all around
even in a two-room apartment with walls as white as a wide-screen screen
and room

for a camera crew as well as a bicycle. Two boys and a girl,
as basic as you can get, *Breathless* is on TV tonight, and Angéla

can't make up her mind, except on one thing: *Je veux un enfant.*
It's either a comedy or a tragedy, or both, or else it's a musical

though the music stops when the songs begin. And Jeanne Moreau, herself,
is hanging out at the neighbourhood bar, *moderato*

cantabile. Karina dancing in and out of a sailor suit, the whole film giddily
spinning around repeated close-ups of her smile.

And just as a rose is a rose is a rose is a rose,
she's not only notorious, she is (with a wink) a woman.

Vivre sa vie My Life to Live

1962

VIVRE

But if life is motion, why is it all so posed?
Her face backlit against some windows,
the camera in formal arcs and tracks
framing the back of her head. Detachment,

says the philosopher. And the artist
goes along for the ride, at least until
gunfire stutters across a café
and Nana, too late, runs for her life.

SA

It's hers, it's hers alone. I raise my hand,
I am responsible. Once I was in a film
with Eddie Constantine.

"*Je... Je est un autre.*" I close my eyes,
I am responsible. Once I was in a film
with Brice Parain.

Speech is like a resurrection. I am unhappy,
I am responsible. Once I was in a film
with Anna Karina.

VIE

But it ends in death: of course,
it's a gangster movie, when there's a girl and a gun
what else do you expect? "*Je veux mourir*"
are almost the first words she says in the film.

And the painter paints his Oval Portrait, Poe
-etry in motion, draining her life
in every close-up, every pendulum pan.
His own voice on the soundtrack reading.

—— *Et ta délivrance?*
(Artaud, Falconetti, tears on her cheek
silent as a silent movie.)
—— *La mort!*

Les Carabiniers The Riflemen

And then went down to the ship — Ulysse
et Michel-Ange, with a shitload of firepower,

in the waste land beyond the periphery
where Venus and Cleopatra

read fashion magazines. There is no
history. Even the spoils of war are spoiled:

a battered suitcase of trophies, thin and paper,
floating signifiers, deeds of promise

guaranteed by the King. Who loses the war.

Gift of the brothers' light: projected image of a train
pulling into a station — Michel-Ange

ducks and covers his eyes. Or else a woman bathing:
he jumps into the air to peep over the rim of her tub

then tears down the screen, but the image survives
on the brick wall behind it. There is no victory:

only flags and falling men. Hostages. Partisans.
And the riflemen on their way to heaven.

Le Mépris
Contempt

And then went down to the ship — Jack Palance
giving orders to Ulysses. And Brigitte Bardot

with a book perched cutely on her bare ass —
Michel picks it up, but only to read the title.

I told you I love you, he told her
the day before, totally, tenderly. But now

love is withering into contempt, and they're both
doing their best to hurry it along, under the lens

of the Mediterranean blue. A voyage
in Italy, with Fritz Lang looking on,

the image of patience. Until Ulysses
lifts his sword in welcome to Ithaca,

and to the silence of that wide-screen sea.

Bande à part Band of Outsiders

1964

First you got onto the local train
at Saint Andrews (back then there was still

a direct connection, you didn't even
have to change at the lonely platforms

of Leuchars Junction) across the girders of
the long Tay Bridge, and into

dingy Dundee, crossing its dull
indiscriminate commerce

reaching the corner of the most
inappropriately named

Bonnybank Road, where you turned left
and climbed the steep hill

to the Tivoli Cinema, which
on alternate weeks

showed 1960s soft-core porn
and the latest "art" films from Europe (one

to subsidise the other, with
an upstairs bar to help), and there

for the first time you saw
a movie which carried the credit

                JEANLUC
                CINEMA
                GODARD

and ever since you have maintained
not just the attribution, but

the equation.

Bande à part
Band of Outsiders

1964

Witnessing the death (in translation) of
Romeo and Juliet

Witnessing the death (in translation) of
Billy the Kid

Franz Kafka as Pat Garrett
Arthur Rimbaud as Billy

in this cold suburb, east
of horizon's monotone

grey line of river between
the haunted, frightened trees

where a minute of silence
lasts 40 seconds

or a tour of the Louvre
less than 10 minutes

and from time to time
in gaiety or tenderness

the earth trembles, and three together
dance the Madison

watching each other
watch each other.

Let's meet for ever at the café
called Tout Va Bien

then sail to Mexico for the next
thrilling instalment.

Une femme mariée
A Married Woman

1964

*Fragments of a poem written
in 2010.*

The first words spoken in this movie:
"I don't know."

Then a white hand moving
on a white sheet. Another hand
moves to meet it. Only one
is wearing a ring.

> Pont de Grenelle
> Tour Eiffel
> Pont Bir Hakeim

Scandal rumour pretext.
Serial taxis.

Measurements for the ideal bust:
what does this strange word mean,
"equilateral"?

Uneven hooking of a bra.

The first thing they put in a machine
is memory.

> 3rd step: you give everyone a warning.

A movie at an airport cinema
on concentration camps.
Peruvian serum.

A week later, when we're dead.

If you have to,
change the title.

Alphaville: une étrange aventure de Lemmy Caution

Alphaville: a Strange Adventure of Lemmy Caution

1965

A train at midnight crosses
the Bir Hakeim Bridge. It plunges
into the darkness of Passy.

This is Paris, 1965, and yet it is also
the city of dreadful night, the future
(where no one lives). It is legend,
it is Alphaville.

Zeroville, sneers Lemmy,
and shoots his lighter aflame, evoking
Natasha into the frame
comme un joli sphinx.

Living in the Capital of Pain, where
tears are forbidden
on penalty of death. Another
word in search of definition:
la not *le*
"*conscience.*"
O Bien-aimée...

Then there are guns and trenchcoats,
casual killings,
and Eurydice lost in the computer network.

Alpha Soixante (his ruined voice)
who is made of Time,
who is destroyed by Time.

There is the straight line to be walked
out of the circle. There is something you must say,
you must say it yourself, I can't
say it for you, something you must say
or else you will remain
lost
among the dead of Alphaville.

A train at midnight crosses
the Bir Hakeim Bridge.

Pierrot le fou Pierrot Goes Wild

1965

Crazy clown. Painted blue.

Listen to old Sam Fuller:
cinema is a battleground.
Love, hate, action, violence, death
— in a word, emotion.

And to express that emotion in its purest form
without even "characters."

So she walks, singing, through the white apartment,
stacks of automatic rifles on the wall
beneath the Picasso reproductions
and a man collapsed on the bed, a pair of scissors
stuck in his neck.

They leave Paris by a one-way street
driving south into Rimbaud's blue.

A weekend crash on a ruined highway.
A poet named after a gun.
Words have the power to disperse the shadows
from around the objects they name.

Wading knee-deep upriver.
Driving a stolen white convertible
into the Mediterranean Sea.

A song stuck in your head
for days and weeks. My name is Ferdinand.

Poetry means loser wins.
Fumbling for the sputter of the fuse.

Crazy clown. Painted blue.

Masculin féminin Masculine Feminine

1966

Nervous, he flips the cigarette
onto his lips, then glances sideways,
letting the famous lock of hair
fall to his forehead. He writes down quotations,

and plays the crackling pinball maze, calls
for a woman to close the café door
before she shoots her husband. He glances again
this time at the girl, and asks her name

not knowing that this story already
has its final scene, and the one to die
abruptly, off-screen, in casual dismissal
this time will be him. Not even in a red sports car —

this movie is in black and white. The children
of Marx and Coca-Cola. Give us this day
a television and a car, but deliver us
from liberty. You cannot live, he tells her,

without tenderness. She opens her eyes
as she lies in the darkness, three in a bed,
and her eyes are all the darkness he needs to know.
So here we are, she tells him, against death.

Masculin féminin
Masculine Feminine

We often went to the movies,
Madeleine and I. When the screen
lit up, we felt a thrill.

But we were often disappointed,
Madeleine and I. The images
seemed dated, they staggered and jumped

right out of the frame. Marilyn Monroe
was showing her age, terribly. We felt sad,
Madeleine and I. Once again it wasn't

the movie of our dreams, that total movie
we carried inside ourselves, that movie
we would have loved to make

or, more secretly no doubt, that movie
we would have loved to live,
Madeleine and I.

Made in USA

Le bonheur, par example...

Here she lies with her dark hair spread over happiness.
There is, for example, a book in her hands as she lies,
perhaps on a bed. Alone. No, it is not in her hands;
the book lies open over her breast. Happiness is in her
hands. She looks to her right. Her right hand holds a
strand of her hair, which is spread over perhaps a pillow.
A book lies over her breast. Her dress is happiness.
The book is called *Adieu la vie, adieu l'amour*. Her eyes
look into happiness: it is far away. Soon she will wear
a trenchcoat, carry a gun. Her dress has a pattern of
large squares: dark red, dark purple, dark happiness.
You can kiss tomorrow goodbye. Her dark hair spreads.
Goodbye to life, goodbye to love, lies over her right
breast. Her right hand holds a strand of dark hair
spread. It is spread over where she is lying. A bed, for
example, or happiness. Do you remember happiness?
Just for example, long ago. There won't be any more,
until the future. Here she lies with her dark hair spread
over happiness; the book lies open on her breast. Her
lover is dead. Her lover is dead, and the search begins,
always already, here.

... oh Paula, you have robbed me of my youth

... oh David, tristesse

Made in USA
1966

Deux ou trois choses que je sais d'elle
Two or Three Things That I Know About Her
1967

If I speak
of a time
it's not yet here

If I speak
of a place
it has already
disappeared

If I speak
of time itself
it's gone
without a trace

And if I speak
of a man
he will soon
be dead

The categories
Left and Right
are obsolete

We must speak of them
otherwise

How then?

The car continues
down
the autoroute

A cup
of coffee swirls
in a spiral
nebula

It is the wide
screen universe

on the table
before you

closer and
closer

Something
may make me cry
but the cause of my tears
is not to be found
in the traces
they leave on my cheeks

I have to
listen
now more than ever
I have to look around me
at the world

It is all here

Mon semblable
mon frère

Deux ou trois choses
que je sais d'elle

Two or Three Things
That I Know About Her
1967

You can hear his voice, it is his, in a whisper
always in your ear

And her voice too, all their voices, interior
insistent monologues

Speak as though quoting the truth
said Papa Brecht

while construction machines tear down
said Papa Haussmann

Language is the house we live in
highrise

Me, in a word? — Indifference

And Buster Keaton upside down

No, not that
The things she will not do
the limits of Pan Am capitalism

Listen to her child's
dream about Vietnam

People never really talk in movies
I wanted to talk with you

But all these signs around us
make me doubt even language
They submerge me in meanings
drowning the real

Me, in a word? — Not yet dead

There is no mystery

It's 4.45pm. Must we speak
he whispers
of Juliette, or of the leaves?
It seems we can't do both at once
Can we?
So let's just say that the two of them
together trembled softly
on this late October
afternoon

La chinoise The Chinese Woman

1967

We are the discourse of others
We are quotations from a little red book

We have painted the walls and the shutters
red white and blue
the windows too

We are what we did
on our summer vacation

We are students and teachers
We write on the blackboards
We have abolished exams

We try to speak pure words
erasing all history

  — On the river
  — Green and blue
  — Tenderness
  — Perhaps
  — Literary theory
  — A film by Nicholas ... Ray
  — The Moscow trials
  — Robin redbreast
  — Rock ... and roll
  — You know I love you

We must confront / vague ideas
with clear / images

Most people don't realize things yet
We must do their thinking
for them

If you make a mistake
and kill the wrong man
then just go back
and kill the right one

Saint-Just will appear
in the time of resurrection
La rentrée

Weekend

> *Prisoner of the Desert* calling
> *Johnny Guitar*

here on the banks of the liberated rivers
in the revolutionary months

> *Pluviôse*
> *Thermidor*

here at the end of story
end of cinema

with all our automobiles burning
with all our faces painted blood

the ordinary carnage of the roads
the lethal plots that sometimes fail

the sports car wrecked
and the Hermès scarf

> Saint-Just in the open fields
> singing into a telephone

My African brother speaks for me

> ACTION MUSICALE
> the circle that completes
> what it cannot express
> and reverses itself

What a rotten film
All we meet are crazy people
eating each other

end of story
end of cinema

> *Johnny Guitar* calling
> *Prisoner of the Desert*

I salute you
old Ocean

Le Gai savoir
Joyful Wisdom; The Gay Science
1968–69

Gay, that is, in the old sense: merry, joyful. "Le gai savoir" is the modern French form of *gai saber*, the Provençal name for the art of poetry, as propounded by a guild formed in 1323, "The Very Gay Company of the Seven Troubadours of Toulouse."

Le Gai Savoir was actually shot in December 1967/January 1968, but not edited and completed until more than a year later — after, that is, the events of May 68. So it both looks forward to these events, and looks back on them. It is full of the anticipation of a revolution to come; it is full of the tragedy of a revolution that has failed. Godard had seen its coming; now he must watch its going.

But for Godard, the discourse of politics is also the "gay science" of poetry. The student of politics is an apprentice troubadour.

One of the slogans painted on the wall of the apartment in *La Chinoise* was: "We must confront vague ideas with clear images." Godard has always produced brilliant images (*Le Gai Savoir* is full of them), but now he begins an intensive self-interrogation of what makes an image not only clear but *true*.

"An image is never an image," the film advances at one point, in a formula worthy of Ezra Pound, "but a contradiction of images." Two images held in dynamic tension. Years later, Godard will find (and repeat, incessantly) a passage in which the poet and art-critic Pierre Reverdy describes that dynamic relation as "both distant and true." Often, also, that contradiction will be between image and sound. "I am 84 years old," proclaims Juliette Berto gaily. "I'm 10.57 metres tall. I'm wearing a yellow jumper" — when we all can see that it's blue.

As usual in Godard, the film is full of quotations. One, obviously added by Godard at the editing stage, after May '68, is a slogan chanted at the occupied Sorbonne in support of the student leader Daniel Cohn-

Bendit, "Danny the Red," who had been attacked in the right-wing press both because he was part-German and because he was a Jew: "Nous sommes tous des juifs allemands," chanted the French students. "We are all German Jews." The Canadian writer Mavis Gallant found this slogan the most important and morally uplifting event of the whole month.

Another quotation is almost invisible; I saw it only when I froze the frame on my DVD. Godard quotes a line from Che Guevera: "At the risk of seeming absurd, I would like to say that the actions of a revolutionary are akin to the act of love." The final phrase is accompanied, on screen, by an erotic drawing of a man and woman making love. In the bottom corner, in tiny lettering, is the inscription "A mon cher Guillaume."

> Picasso.
> To Apollinaire.
> The art of poetry.
> Le gai savoir.

One Plus One
a.k.a. Sympathy for the Devil
1968

Please allow me to introduce myself

I run a soft-core pornographic bookstore in London
and I read to my customers
chapters from *Mein Kampf*

I am a Black Panther in a wrecked car lot
and I read to my victims
white and female
the speeches of Eldridge Cleaver

I am Eve Democracy, and having that name
I can respond to questions
only by referendum
only by Yes or No[1]

I am Mick Jagger, worker in song, and
baffled by sound
on the road to Altamont

One Plus One
is never finished

The red flag and the black flag fly
from a camera crane as it soars to the sky

------

[1] As in:

—   Is it true that there is only one way
       to be an intellectual revolutionary
       and that is to stop being an intellectual?
—   Yes.

British Sounds
a.k.a. See You at Mao

1969

British sounds, or
just B S

The scream of metal on the assembly line
The workers' voices in their daily grousing
The child repeating history lessons

Always, the image against the sound
stretching out the contradictions

Nude descending a staircase
full frontal shot
defying the gaze

defying you to switch attention
to the feminist commentary

"Don't you think I can make a cunt boring?"

Struggling to change
the lyrics of a song

Struggling to change
the lyrics of a state

And the blood-stained hand
over barren ground
that reaches for the blood-stained banner
to raise it high

"Don't you think I can make a red flag boring?"

Pravda
Dziga Vertov Group

1969

Beloved comrade Rosa

I send you some pictures and some sound
of a country which has not yet had
its revolution

a country occupied by tanks
and by American advertisements

and of students who in 1968
danced through the spring

I send you a red rose

Beloved comrade Vladimir

I send you some pictures and some sound
from the Kennedy-Khruschev class alliance

You do not understand Czech

The workers talk like Henry Ford
        not like Black Panthers
The students talk like Newsweek
        not like Tom Hayden
The peasants talk like a mid-West farmer
        not like a Los Angeles chicano

We must add true sound to false pictures
to find a true picture again

Our voices stumble as we read our texts
we do not edit the recording
all the false starts remain

Beloved comrade Vladimir
Beloved comrade Rosa

I send you a red flag
mounted on a truck as it drives
through an occupied country

Vent d'est Wind from the East

Dziga Vertov Group
1969

Here's the irony:

all I have left
of this film

    Wind from the East
     the clarifying wind
     the revolution's hurricane

all I have left
is a skuzzy videotape
the visuals so degraded
there is nothing to be seen

out of focus images
illegible signs
fifth generation copy

but the sound
    — Death to Bourgeois Culture! —
but the sound
    — Reflect. Simplify. Wait. Learn. —
but the sound
    — "those who poisoned the horses" —
but the sound

is as clear as a bell. And just
as dogmatic.

The hectoring, lecturing voice
has won its final victory
over the stubborn, persistent
ambiguity
of the visual.

I eject the VHS tape,
slot it back in its box,
file it back on its shelf,

open my window, and listen
for a wind from the east.

Lotte in Italia Struggles in Italy

Dziga Vertov Group
1970

Paola stares at the camera
raising her right hand in
clenched-fist salute. We see her

reading several newspapers, one
headline at a time, or
crossing lines out of a manuscript, or
eating her soup.

She tries on clothes, which are
very plain. She opens a window
onto a balcony, but only
to close a shutter.

Backlit, corona of her hair
clings like a creature to her skull.

> The sound track is not
> translated: still
> I can make out some of the words.

> Revisionism.
> Theory and Practice.
> Work and Struggle.

Sometimes the whole screen fills
with a blazing red.

Vladimir et Rosa
Vladimir and Rosa

Dziga Vertov Group
1971

It is the voice that sees

that asks, observes, arraigns, produces,
prosecutes, knows.

It is the Chicago trial, the group of 8,
replayed in Paris, under the screeching dwarf —
objection denied! — Judge Himmler.

Pig circus.

Here is the Group, Jean-Luc and Jean-Pierre,
mixed doubles going on around them.
One holds the mike / the other wears headphones.
The sound of their dialogue
volleying the net
emerges on a tape delay, the words
are echoing stutters, but they

know which way the wind blows.

The lawyer rehearses his closing argument,
dramatic courtroom gestures.
"I say my lines before the audience hears them.
What it hears will be in the past."
And the defendants recite their sentences
before they receive them.

Some of us are prisoners.
The rest of us are guards.

In 1971
it is the voice that sees.

Tout va bien It's all good

with Jean-Pierre Gorin

1972

You had your motorcycle crash
just like Bob Dylan's

but hey, don't worry,
it's all good

                                        The fact is

You've got your big-time movie stars
who are worried

whether or not there's a spotlight
on the back of their ears

                                        the truth is simple

but hey, don't worry, it's someone else
who's signing the cheques

someone else who is painting
the whole wall blue
even the paintings

                                        but it's not simple

And these are the problems
four years later:

what it slowly means
every day
to be a captive

                                        to tell the truth

what it slowly means
every day
to be free

                But don't you worry:
                Tout va bien.
                It's all good.

Letter to Jane

with Jean-Pierre Gorin

1972

there is a soundtrack

LETTER TO JANE

which poses questions
to which there are already

LETTER TO JANE

answers the questions: why

LETTER TO JANE

are you frowning? what
part are you playing?
and are you asking

LETTER TO JANE

the questions we might have
asked you to ask? and
why does it take us

LETTER TO JANE

fifty minutes of angry speech
to counteract

LETTER TO JANE

one moment of you in your cute
Klute hairdo, leaving you

LETTER TO JANE

no chance to respond?

Numéro deux Number Two

Screen within screen: video monitor
inside the 35 emulsion. Number One /

Number Two. A simultaneous montage
within the static frame. It's just another language and,
after all, it's love that taught us language.

And so, a family: three dying generations
at their song. Before I was born, I was dead.

We see the hole where memory comes from.
Where does it go?

Mum and Dad: the factory, the countryside:
but which is which? And which is
Number Two?

Grandpa reciting trade union memories;
Grandma reciting Germaine Greer.

What we're never allowed to see
is the little boy's penis:
the future's secrecy.

But we do see
Jeannot's hands on the volume controls
playing them like a pianist.

Number One.

Comment ça va? How's It Going?

1976

It's not just the words between them,
faltered, repeated ideas — like

"Franco is dead" or
"Twenty thousand men in uniform"

It's the machines that the words
enter and exit — what happens to them in there?

It's the way that both hands shift
over a typewriter keyboard,

the way the eyes move, darting
around a photograph, or sliding

left and right along lines of text. How's it going?
where from? and where to? Liberation?

She says this, and he listens impatiently.
She says this, but we never see her face.

Outside is a winter landscape, cars on icy corners,
a couple who watch their kids play football

and seldom speak. Outside is Spain,
and the bosses who decide.

Inside, there are words, and machines,
and a thousand questions, all in uniform.

Sauve qui peut (la vie)
Every Man for Himself,
a.k.a. Slow Motion
1980

The sky a blue so intense
the only word is "azure."

And then the bicycle — slow movement
filmed in slow motion. Stop, stop,

and start again. Rimbaud
on her way to Godard.

What is that music that I hear?
sometimes there, or not, on the soundtrack,

sometimes on the street beside me,
heard without paying attention.

C'est pas triste. It's not a tragedy.
It's always the last time until it's the next.

(Duras in the back seat, in absentia):
when you see a truck passing

think of it as the word of a woman
passing. The silence that always surrounds

the reading of a text. My landlady says:
"I don't feel like having ideas

nowadays." You want a guardian angel
and I'm through being one.

I want to do things, not define them —
I leave the definitions to you.

Commerce. Violence. Humiliation.
Above all, humiliation. Show me, show me.

Sex on a bizarre assembly line. The orchestra
is there, is truly there, in the alley

soundtrack for a death. Mother and daughter
walking away. Slow motion.

Passion

Tableaux vivants — the actors,
fidgeting a little, unconcerned by nakedness,
com/posed in real three dimensions —

Old Master paintings, reproduced
(Rembrandt, Velasquez, Delacroix)
by a younger master — but what does it mean

"to reproduce"? Assembly line production
like in a factory, where cinema is
forbidden? Are love and work

a single image, "distant and true" (Reverdy
making his first appearance)? The boss
with persistent cough and a rose between his teeth

or the German hotel-owner watching herself
in the Polish director's video. Speak your line!
Agnus Dei — Requiem. I wish

I could have loved you
with a passion. But in the end
everyone is going home —

to Poland, to Hollywood, or on
a sailing ship set in a snow-ridged field,
Watteau. The embarkation for Cythera.

Scénario du film Passion
Screenplay for the film Passion
1982

Not just the usual
ravings of Jean-Luc —
seated at his editing board,
before him the white screen

which is a Berlin wall
made for jumping over;
the screen is a rupture,
a lapse in memory.

Can we ever see the Law?
Did Moses have to
have it in writing?
Can the screenplay be seen
before it's a script?

Writing, so they say, began with
merchants — before
Madame Bovary or *Libération*
there was the inscription of
a load delivered,
three kilos of carrots.

I should burn my eyes with images
in order to see them, distant and true.

And music, ah music — for ever Mozart
I bought at the airport. Duty free.
Music is my Antigone.

What's left at the end is metaphor —

the only way to arrive at reality,
the only way to bring it all back home.

Prénom Carmen
First Name: Carmen

1983

A train at midnight crosses
the Bir Hakeim Bridge
again. And again. Two trains

in opposite directions, insistent
as a musical motif
in a Beethoven string quartet,

or the waves that break on the shore. Continuity.
I'll make a note.
I'll explain it to you later.

The world does not belong to the innocent.
Oh little soldier. Joseph, impotently
jerking his prick in the shower,

failing to understand.
"If I love you, that's the end of you,"
as they said in that American movie.

What comes first, before the name?
Van Gogh went looking for yellow
when the sun disappeared.

Uncle Jean, with Buster Keaton
upside down on his knees.
Tapping the room for every sound.

And all that random gunfire. Continuity.
I'll make a note.
I'll explain it to you later.

What's it called, when everything's lost
and we're still breathing? Mademoiselle,
it's called the dawn.

Le livre de Marie
The Book of Mary

Anne-Marie Miéville
1985

TAKE ONE

Absolutely lucid light: her balcony
gives onto Lac Léman, as clear as any
equation in geometry, her father
with a tired face tries to explain.

Sweet as an apple in a still life bowl:
her mother's face, and the slow
wearing away of contempt in the background,
family life on a regular
schedule of trains. Her own name,

Marie, in which we can also read
Aimer: who is there to love
but the absent father, the present mother,
immaculate, the lucid light
on the ruins of her balcony?

TAKE TWO

Absolutely lucid light, on the ruins
of your balcony, Lac Léman,
a voice singing la la la
like the Rhinemaidens' song.
And the slow repeated argument,
no voices raised, the scenes of Contempt
play only in the background, on TV.
In front of the TV set, an apple.

Sweet as an apple in a bowl, in a painting,
Chardin or Cézanne, so sweet you could eat it
or slice it open, as if it were Bunuel's eye,
implant a pupil, roll it round. Silence, I said,
silence. Listen to Baudelaire.
Or dance to the final symphony,
pulling your punches, tossing your hair.

Marie, there are four kinds of triangle,
and the sides are never equal. He walks with you
on a street in Geneva; he says goodbye.
You cut the top off an egg
as if it were the whole of Europe.
You admire your mother's dark dress.
Your name is an anagram of Love.

Je vous salue, Marie Hail Mary

1985

It's not a blessing, it's a command
as rude and abrupt
as a fuck you in the face of God.

My belly bulges like a basketball
to the cut-throat visitation
of hoodlum angels. Annunciation

between the gas pumps. Only
the sad-sack professor gets to get out of here,
rationalising paradise. While Joseph

carpenter and taxi-driver
only goes where he is told to go,
with no direction home.

I must learn to write
if I want to forget. What we're speaking of,
the Word, is always ahead of us.

I am the victim of time,
which takes its own sweet time to consume me
as I twist the bed-sheets in agony

under the sun-shattered sky,
under the blessing of rain,

while God like a cloud of anger
fills my room.

Détective Detective

Le Prince d'Aquitaine à la tour abolie

Princess, don't you know
the Prince is dead
and history keeps repeating itself
in a long stutter

in a long stutter, like a technical knock out
recorded on Agfa cassette
advertised in neon on the roof
of a grand Parisian hotel

— for all great cities,
Lord, are accursed

We're not in some small French film
where the actors believe
that talking is thinking
This is a big money production
with actors and stars

This is a big money deal
and he who dies in a tempest
pays all debts

The shootings are, as always,
accidental

To be a witness means
to be a martyr

Soft and Hard: Soft Talk on a Hard Subject
between Two Friends

Jean-Luc Godard and Anne-Marie Miéville
1985

This is hard to say:
cinema will die soon, very young,
without having given everything it could.

The two of them sit
on soft cushions, at right angles,
each has to twist
to see the other. His back is to the camera.

Still looking for the road to the Word,
she does the ironing.
He plays tennis.

In dreams (he says) several
directors are at work.
Northern dreams (she says)
are paler and more violent.
If I have made images (he says)
instead of children, does that make me
any less human?

Your problem is (she says) you can't write dialogue
for love scenes. He's trying, not always successfully,
not to interrupt her.

The dialogue ends where contempt begins:
shadow of arms on a wall, the camera
turning to face the audience.

The project of becoming a subject:
where has it gone, oh
where has it gone?

It's hard to say.

Soigne ta droite: une place sur la terre
Keep Your Right Up: A Place on the Earth
1987

What happens next is from long ago

At the end of the 20th century
the Idiot's telephone rings

And what follows is slapstick, Buster Godard,
it takes him five minutes
to fall into a car

      Meanwhile there is music being made

Giving the ultimate gift: your own
poisoned pill
to another's hand
just before atrocity

It's always sad to leave the earth

      Don't forget your little shoes
      Don't forget to tie them tight

Somehow, the plane takes off, though the pilot
is reading a how-to book on suicide
and the passengers, led by the flight attendant, chant
as if on a weekend singalong
"I salute you, old ocean"

      You need to adjust the drum machine

There is a child behind a door
and the door closes
and the door opens
onto a balcony, onto a lake
No need to make this into tragedy
C'est pas triste

Actors don't like to make appearances
They prefer disappearances

I fear I am not in my perfect mind

> Of course the song is never finished:
> One Plus One

Somehow, the plane lands
the film is delivered (the toughest thing in cinema
is carrying the cans)

and the Idiot dies — it's in the back
that the light stabs darkness

What happens next is from long ago

King Lear

I fear I am not in my perfect mind.

Fathers and daughters, daughters and fathers —
blood on the sheets, blood on the tracks
of desire.

The famous writer and his daughter,
speaking their lines, then flying away —
love, and be silent.

A violent silence —
the silence of Cordelia,
who says nothing. No thing. O

what dear daughter? After Chernobyl
the rediscovery
of the ancestor's text — fragments I have shored,

quotations on the Wall. *Le roi Lire*.
While in the woods,
the Fool with a head like Medusa's, sprouting

video cables, twists his speech
out of the sidelong corners
of his mouth. Saint John. Saint Luke.

Evangelists. And always the image,
distant and true,
in the time of resurrection.

Lear on the beach at daybreak,
his long gun held on guard,
Cordelia's body on a rock behind him,

waiting
as the dawn bleeds
over the waves of Lac Léman.

> And in me too the wave rises…
> Percival, when he galloped in India

So here we are, she tells him, against death.

> Why, then, she lives.

Nouvelle vague New Wave

1990

I wanted this to be a narrative.

So finally Jean-Luc went all the way:
every line in the script
a quotation from somewhere else.
Every blessed line.

Love doesn't die.
It's people who die.
Love just goes away.

The gardener on his John Deere tractor
orates in ornate poetry.

A garden, like prose,
is never finished.
Certain gardens are described as retreats
when they should be called attacks.

OK, so there is a narrative. About a man
who dies, and is reborn,
and dies, and is reborn.

For the first time
we have the chance
to say things
for the last time.
French syntax is incorruptible.

The long horizontal
tracking shot
outside the windows of the house
each room
lit by a gold warm lamp.

Memory is the only paradise
we can't be expelled from.

And then the reverse track
as a woman passes from room to room
extinguishing the lamps.

The night is rising.

But doesn't night fall?

No, no, the night is rising.

Allemagne année 90 neuf zero
Germany Year 90 Nine Zero
1991

So it's Lemmy again
in the same
trenchcoat and hat

25 years later, playing
the last secret agent
in a country
where all the spies are dead

but it's Germany still
haunting old Europe
His face is in shadows

as he asks Don Quixote
which way it is
to the West

but "as soon as I crossed the border
I met the ghosts"

and then there was only another
strange adventure:
a hotel maid reciting
"*Arbeit macht frei*"

while she makes up his bed
as innocently
as if she was still
25 years later
living in Alphaville

Hélas pour moi Alas for me

1993

Woe is all Greek to me, you
two-faced arrogant Gods, playing
games with your family names.

A messenger arrives, a plodding
raincloud trudging down the road. While "Italy,"
the white boat sliding softly
past petrified figures, on Lac Léman, announces:

Five days ago I learned that it is possible
for the flesh to be sad. So what good is desire
if you need a body?

Swim into focus. Fade into blue. Invasion of images
into the ordinary. What do you do
when the God who attacks you smiles, or tries to,
with a familiar face?

And Ludovic died in Dubrovnik
having left his home from a station
where the trains roar by
without stopping.

JLG / JLG: *autoportrait de décembre*
JLG / JLG: Self-Portrait in December
1995

It begins like this: when death arrives
in December, Frimaire,

storms on the lakeshore, opposite
the Kingdom of France

and pools of warm light
in darkened rooms.

I was already in mourning, he says,
for myself, my sole companion

and there seems to be
no one else in the house.

This is the legend of stereo.
JLG / JLG:

Johnny Luc Guitar
tramping through shallows

or playing winter tennis
on a covered court.

This slow, snow-covered landscape.
And then the Inspectors come

and the blind film editor
chopping the frames.

Where do you live?
In language, and I cannot keep quiet.

An old woman steals my coat
and recites Virgil.

If there is truth in the mouths of poets,
I shall live.

For Ever Mozart

One doesn't trifle with love
in Sarajevo. It's as if

the innocents of 68 had been reborn,
clumsily, thirty years later, without a cause,

so they chose Yugoslavia.
And instead of a little red book,

a volume of classic French comedy.
But the riflemen are still there

and if you've got so many guns
you have to shoot somebody.

In the ruined house, before their death, they inspect
old measurements, quotations on the wall.

Meanwhile the old man turns away, hitches a ride
back to his solitude. A director

with nothing to direct. Some lines
of porno dialogue, and a windswept beach.

A woman in a red gown outside a window,
her words lost in the howling storm.

Let's keep it simple, he says to her.
You try to say Yes, and I will always

answer No.

(But then there's Mozart, isn't there? For ever Mozart.
The old man hunches at the head of the stair,

and his hands keep time.)

Histoire(s) du cinéma
History(ies) of Cinema
1998

(1)

Change nothing
so that everything is different.

Two finger typing.
All the stories.

Art is like fire,
born from what it burns.

I am the mistake that lives.

The image will appear
in the time of resurrection.

Cinema: the industry of masks,
or, a minor branch
of the industry of lies.

Cinema: the only place
where memory is a slave.

Trade follows film.

Cogito Ergo Video.
Histoire(s) with an S.
SS.

Cinema authorizes Orpheus to look back
without the death of Eurydice.
Debbie, let's go home.

Perspective was the original sin of European painting:
Niépce and Lumière were its redeemers.

Man has in his poor heart
places that do not yet exist
and into which pain enters
in order for them to exist.

What I like in cinema:
a saturation of magnificent signs
bathing in the light
of their absence of explanation.

But first Elpenor came.

(1a)

Lie to me.
> The Law of Silence (I Confess).
>> *If it be your will.*

A man is punting a boat on a river.
> *Tell me that all these years you've waited.*
>> The Pursuit of Happiness.

Then the whispering resumes.
> *All these years I've waited.*
>> *That I speak no more.*

Voyage with No Return.
> A couple approach an abandoned house.
>> A telephone rings. Hullo?

Tell me you'd have died if I hadn't come back.
> Sauve Qui Peut (La Vie).
>> A photograph of Henri Langlois.

I will speak no more.
> *I would have died if you hadn't come back.*
>> Man with a Movie Camera.

Out of a dust-storm, Johnny rides in to Vienna's.
> *I shall abide until.*
>> *Tell me that you still love me like I love you.*

I still love you like you love me.
> Leonard Cohen. Nicholas Ray.
>> *If it be your will.*

Eloge de l'amour
In Praise of Love

Paris again. High contrast:
black and white, the headlights flare

into the lens. And on a bench, he's reading
a book of blank pages. Audition /

interrogation. A woman with a freckled,
astonished face. Eglantine:

remember the names? She says No.

And the relics, factory remains
of Renault, 1968, the empty shells

across the river, memory denied.

America, she tells us, has no history,
has no name. All it can do

is buy another, second hand. Resistance
copyright by Steven Spielberg. What we want

is *Matrix* with the soundtrack dubbed
into Breton. Two years before, and

two years after: *The Voyage of Edgar*
laid on a café table, legacy. She went

to Amsterdam: they know
how to arrange things there.

She lives in shadows, will not give
her name or address. A train pulls away

from the future.

Notre musique Our Music

First Kingdom is Hell: war
and all the images of war:
the infinite variety we have created
of ways to kill each other, and then
tell stories about the killing. But
killing a man to defend an idea
doesn't defend the idea, it only
kills a man.

Second Kingdom: Purgatory
turns out to be an academic conference
in Sarajevo. Books piled on the floor
of the ruined Library. Snow. Some writers
looking for the missing poet
of defeated Troy. Scaffolding around
the broken bridge at Mostar. And Olga running
towards her own destruction: the land;
the promise; the atonement.
I bear the obedient language
like a cloud.

Third Kingdom: Paradise
a lakeshore guarded by US Marines,
the point of no return.
Oh David, tristesse.

Film socialisme Film Socialism

(1) .

So, money is a public good.
Like water? Exactly — like the wave
that breaks on the bow. One time

I encountered the void — oh well,
it's much, much smaller
than you might believe.

Someone is crying on the upper deck
"Abandon ship!" But no one listens
and the ship sails on.
The strobe light strobes.

War criminals lounge along the railing.
Patti Smith is singing in the bar,
wearing white trousers.
There is a knife, and a war, and

something cut off. There are questions of gold,
where it came from, where it went.
There are ports of call.

(2)

There is a garage, which is up for sale.
Three dying generations, at their song.

And what if some of us just kids
ran for President?
A TV crew is here to record

all the divisions. Please don't use
the verb "to be." Why don't you love us?
Something to do with the law

of common right — 1789,
Saint-Just encore
in a weekend field. A service station

where Mary and Joseph meet
and an infant paints Renoir,
before the future.

(3)

Cruise ship, history as tourism,
all of the Mediterranean
under an azure sky. Infection setting in.

Joan Baez sings for Abraham
an anti-war song, in German, holding on
to a flying trapeze.

The haunted face of Simone Weil
in Tarantula lighting,
playing a mother carrying a child

on the Odessa Steps.
And then the director's final word
protected by the F B I:

When the law is not just
then justice comes
before the law.

     NO COMMENT

     Lie to me

     NO COMMENT

À bout de souffle Breathless

1960–2010

Imagine then Belmondo, at the limit of breath,
in his first landscape, on his final street

imagine he glimpses visions
distant and true

of all the images that are to come:

    his own blue stupid death
    Karina's face
    Karina's face
    Saint-Just in a weekend field
    a red flag waving
    the passion of a living painting
    absolutely sweet Marie
    a game of tennis in winter
    an ocean liner on a crystal sea

Lie to me, he whispers,
tell me that you've always loved me

But all she can say in reply is still

What does it mean?
What does that strange word mean?

Notes

For over fifty years, Jean-Luc Godard has been one of the leading
figures in world cinema; many people (including me) would say that
he is the greatest film director of his age. Although he is still most
widely identified with the early years of the French New Wave, the early
1960s, Godard's career is remarkable for its persistence and longevity.
Throughout his later decades, he has continued to make films which
challenge, like no others, the most fundamental aspects of cinematic
narrative and language, while still producing images of piercing clarity
and beauty.

My own fascination with Godard began in 1965, with the first movie
of his I ever saw: *Bande à Part* (the circumstances of that first viewing
are recorded on pages 9–10). It has continued unabated ever since, even
through the "difficult" years of his political cinema.

In this book, I set myself the goal of celebrating Godard by writing
poems based on his films: one poem for each film, written and
presented in chronological order. I made it a condition that I should
re-view each film before writing about it. Over the years, I have
accumulated a near-complete collection of Godard on v H S and D V D
(even if some of the more dubiously acquired copies are of wretched
visual quality). I am missing several of the films from the political
period: *Un film comme les autres* (1968), *One American Movie* (1968), and
Ici et Ailleurs (1974). Of the later titles, the major omission is *Grandeur et
décadence d'un petit commerce de cinéma* (1986). I have for the most part
omitted Godard's short films, as well as sketches he contributed to
compilation films by several directors; nor have I attempted to deal with
most of his very extensive work for television. I did include the short
film *Letter to Jane*, co-directed with Jean-Pierre Gorin, and also Anne-
Marie Miéville's short film, *Le livre de Marie*, which is an integral part of
the package release of *Je vous salue, Marie* (see page 83, notes to pages
47–49). Mainly, however, the poems deal with the theatrically released
features. The general rule was one poem per film, but a few exceptions
did enforce themselves.

The poems are closely keyed to the films. Most of the poetic
images are taken from the film in question, and I quote extensively
from the soundtrack dialogue. Such quotation is one of Godard's own

fundamental techniques: his films are full of other people's words, sometimes openly acknowledged, frequently not. Godard has filmed more images of people reading than any other ten directors combined. (For an extended discussion of this topic, in relation to Godard and also to one of my other idols, Bob Dylan, see my essay "Plagiarism, Bob, Jean-Luc, and Me," published in the proceedings of the conference "Refractions of Bob Dylan," University of Vienna, 2011.)

The poems will thus be most fully appreciated by readers who have seen the films. But my hope is that the images and ideas will still have force even for those who are not familiar with their sources.

The following Notes make no attempt to account for all of the quotations I make from Godard's dialogue; the reader can assume that any given poem contains a number of lines drawn from the film being written about. I have tried to account for some of the major echoes from sources other than Godard himself (especially Dylan). As to the use to which I put such quotations, the extent to which I make of them something new or different, readers must judge for themselves.

p. v   People in love
This quotation is adapted from *Godard on Godard*, trans. Tom Milne, New York, 1972, page 173. In the original, the first line reads "People in life quote as they please." I mistyped "life" as "love" (no doubt a significant slip); but when I eventually discovered my error, I had grown so fond of the misquoted version that I decided to let it stand.

p. VII   An image
This passage is freely adapted and translated from the writing of the French poet and critic Pierre Reverdy. It first appeared in his magazine *Nord-Sud*, number 13, March 1918. The later Godard seized upon it almost as a manifesto. It appears first in *Passion* (1982), and is quoted in several other films, most extensively in *King Lear* (1987).

p. 1   at the limit of breath
Richard Brody, in his definitive biography of Godard, *Everything Is Cinema* (New York: Metropolitan Books, 2008), writes: "To be precise, *A bout de souffle* should be translated as 'Out of Breath': 'Breathless' has a positive quality of joyful astonishment or satiety with pleasure that is

absent from 'à bout de souffle,' which refers to a state of exhaustion"
(page 638). I am indebted to Brody for providing the source for several
other citations in these Notes.

p. 1   pointing you the way to go
Bob Dylan, "Tears of Rage." For the comparison between Godard and
Dylan, see my essay, cited above, "Plagiarism, Bob, Jean-Luc, and Me,"
which includes the following summary: "Both [Dylan and Godard] burst
on the scene in the early 60s as the *enfants terribles* of their arts; both
of them survived motorcycle accidents, Dylan in 1966 and Godard in
1971; both of them went through periods of extreme ideological rigidity,
Godard with Maoism and Dylan with evangelical Christianity; both of
them are problematic, to say the least, in their depiction of women;
both of them emerged to produce some of their finest work in the fourth
or fifth decades of their careers." Dylan therefore figures as a persistent
sub-text in these poems.

In the film, the anonymous man in the street who points out to
the police the way to go to follow the fugitive Belmondo is played, in a
Hithcockian gesture, by Godard himself.

p. 2   Which side are you on?
1931 Trade Union song by Florence Reece. Quoted by Dylan in
"Desolation Row."

p. 2   By the waters of Leman
As used by T.S. Eliot in *The Waste Land*, Part III: "By the waters of
Leman I sat down and wept," adapted from Psalm 137, where it reads
"By the rivers of Babylon, there we sat down, yea, we wept, when we
remembered Zion."

"Leman," without the French accent, is an old English word for lover
or sweetheart. "Lac Léman," with the accent, is the French name for
Lake Geneva. *Le Petit Soldat* is set in Geneva. Later in his career, when he
settled in Rolle, Switzerland, images of Lac Léman become a ubiquitous
presence in Godard's films.

p. 2   her Danish hair
Anna Karina, the star of many early Godard films, and also his first wife,
was Danish by birth. The most adored face in 1960s cinema.

p. 2   Lie to me

Opening line of a famous, romantically ironic dialogue exchange between Joan Crawford and Sterling Hayden in *Johnny Guitar* (1954, directed by Nicholas Ray). A favourite moment, frequently quoted by Godard; see also pages 62, 65, 70, 71.

p. 4   Raoul

Raoul Coutard, inventive cinematographer on all Godard's early films.

p. 4   moderato cantabile

As a musical direction: in a moderate time, in a flowing style. Title of a 1958 novel by Marguerite Duras, filmed in 1960, directed by Peter Brook and starring Jeanne Moreau and Jean-Paul Belmondo.

p. 4   a rose is a rose

Motto of Gertrude Stein. For a discussion of the phrase, see Stephen Scobie, *The Measure of Paris* (Edmonton: University of Alberta Press, 2010), pages 151–157. Godard's title puns "une femme," a woman, with "infâme," infamous, notorious.

p. 5   Eddie Constantine

American actor who worked mostly in Europe, where he became a star playing the tough-guy detective Lemmy Caution. Karina does indeed appear alongside him in Godard's *Alphaville* (1965); much later he reappears in *Allemagne Année 90 Neuf Zero* (1991).

p. 5   Je est un autre

"I is another." Phrase used in a letter by the Symbolist poet Arthur Rimbaud, which has become a basic slogan for the modern sensibility.

p. 5   Brice Parain

French philosopher (1897–1971), whose work is chiefly concerned with the nature of language. In *Vivre Sa Vie*, he appears as himself, in dialogue with Nana.

p. 6   Oval Portrait

Story by Edgar Allan Poe, in which a painter's portrait of his wife drains her of life. In the film, the story is read in voiceover by Karina's husband, Godard himself.

p. 6   Et ta délivrance? ... La mort!
From *La Passion de Jeanne d'Arc* (1928), directed by Carl Theodor Dreyer, starring Falconetti and Antonin Artaud.

pp. 7, 8   And then went down to the ship
First line of Ezra Pound's *Cantos*. The implied subject is Ulysses. "Canto I" is later quoted by Godard in *Histoire(s) du Cinéma*: see page 86, note to page 66.

p. 7   brothers' light
The Lumière Brothers, Auguste and Louis, first showed their moving pictures in 1895. One of their first films was *Train Arriving at a Station*, which caused panic among audiences. The scene is reproduced in Martin Scorsese's *Hugo* (2011).

p. 8   A voyage in Italy
1954 film by Roberto Rossellini, hailed as a masterpiece by Godard and the critics of *Cahiers du Cinéma*.

p. 11   haunted, frightened trees
Bob Dylan, "Mr Tambourine Man."

p. 13   Fragments of a poem
Une Femme Mariée bears the subtitle "Fragments of a film shot in 1964."

p. 13   Pont Bir Hakeim
The Bir Hakeim bridge, which crosses the Seine at Passy, is a two-level bridge, with an open-air stretch of the Métro on the upper deck. It is named after a battle in Libya in World War II, in which the Free French forces held off the German army of Rommel. It appears in several Godard movies (*Une Femme Mariée, Alphaville, Prénom Carmen*), and also in the opening scene of Bernardo Bertolucci's *Last Tango in Paris*. I often crossed it at midnight, on the last Métro home to rue Rousselet from the late show at the Cinémathèque.

p. 14   change the title
Under pressure from the French censorship authorities, Godard changed his title from "The" Married Woman (implying a sociological generalization) to "A" Married Woman (implying a specific, non-representative case).

p. 15   city of dreadful night
Title of a dystopian poem by James Thompson (1874).

p. 15   Capital of Pain
Capitale de la douleur (1926) is the most important book by Surrealist
poet Paul Éluard.

p. 15   O Bien-aimée...
Oh well beloved ... a common phrase, but I associate it with Jacques
Derrida, in a passage from *La Carte Postale* (1980), which Douglas
Barbour and I adapted as a performance text for our group,
Re:Sounding.

p. 17   Sam Fuller
American film director, much admired by Godard and the critics of
Cahiers du Cinéma, makes a cameo appearance, as himself, in *Pierrot
le Fou*.

p. 19   We often went to the movies
This poem is adapted from the soundtrack voiceover spoken by Jean-
Pierre Léaud. Godard quotes this passage, almost directly, but without
attribution, from Georges Perec, *Les Choses: une histoire des années
soixante* (1965). Godard's scene is further quoted and adapted by Todd
Haynes in his film on Bob Dylan, *I'm Not There* (2007). For a discussion
of this intertextual maze, see my essay, cited above, "Plagiarism, Bob,
Jean-Luc, and Me."

p. 20   Made in USA
This poem was first written in 1970, and appeared in my book *The Rooms
We Are* (Sono Nis: 1974). It also appeared in *The Spaces In Between: Selected
Poems 1965–2001* (NeWest: 2003).

p. 20   Adieu la vie, adieu l'amour
French title of *Kiss Tomorrow Goodbye*, a thriller by Horace McCoy,
published in 1948, and filmed, with James Cagney, in 1950.

p. 20   David
The character killed by Karina in the penultimate scene is named David
Goodis, after the American thriller writer, very popular in France, whose

best-known work is *Shoot the Piano Player* (1956), filmed in 1960 by François Truffaut. The line *"Oh David, tristesse"* (the name pronounced à la française) is spoken by Karina immediately after she shoots him. See also page 67.

p. 21   *Made in USA / Two or Three Things*
The making of these two films overlapped, so that at one stage, so the story goes, Godard was working on one film in the mornings and the other in the afternoons.

p. 21   *I have to listen…*
This passage from Godard's film is also quoted by Todd Haynes in *I'm Not There*. The quote from Baudelaire ("Mon semblable…"), also used by Eliot in *The Waste Land*, appears at the end of this scene in Godard's film.

p. 22   *Papa Haussmann*
Georges-Eugène Haussmann, Prefect of the Seine region from 1853 until 1870, was largely responsible for the demolition of the old Paris and the reconstruction of the modern city. For a discussion of the pros and cons of his much debated career, see Scobie, *The Measure of Paris*, 9–18.

p. 25   *Saint-Just*
Louis-Antoine Saint-Just (1767–94), one of the youngest and fiercest of the Jacobin leaders of the French Revolution; guillotined on the 10th day of Thermidor, Year II. Played in *La Chinoise* by Jean-Pierre Léaud, who also briefly appears in the part in *Weekend*, a scene which is quoted again, many years later, in *Film Socialisme*. Saint-Just was a figure much admired by the Scottish poet Ian Hamilton Finlay.

p. 25   *the time of resurrection*
See page 84, note to page 54. Godard did not use this phrase until 20 years later, but I have ventured to transpose it back to the context of *La Chinoise*, where it may be read as an ironic translation of "la rentrée."

p. 25   *La rentrée*
Early September: date when French universities and schools re-open, and cultural life generally resumes. End of the summer vacation, in which the characters of the film have been, both literally and metaphorically, living.

p. 26   Prisoner of the Desert

In *Weekend*, the cells of the fantasized hippy revolutionary "Seine and Oise Liberation Front" communicate with each other by 2-way radio, using as call signs the names of American movies beloved by Godard and the critics of *Cahiers du Cinéma*. For *Johnny Guitar*, see page 76, note to page 2. The original English sub-titler of *Weekend* apparently did not realize that *La Prisonnière du Désert* is not some non-existent American film called *Prisoner of the Desert*, but is in fact the French title for John Ford's *The Searchers* (1956), the greatest Western ever made.

p. 27   I salute you / old Ocean

Spoken in the film by the leader of the Seine and Oise Liberation Front, while playing a drum solo in front of a rather placid pond. Quoted (without any attribution in the film) from "Les Chants de Maldoror," by the Comte de Lautréamont (Isidore Ducasse), French Symbolist/Decadent poet, 1846–70. The line recurs, in even more comic form, in *Soigne Ta Droite* (1987) — see page 52.

p. 30   Please allow me to introduce myself

First line of the song "Sympathy for the Devil," by The Rolling Stones. Godard's film shows the Stones at work in the studio, trying out various versions of the song. In Godard's final edit, the song remains unresolved and uncompleted. The English producer, Iain Quarrier, dubbed in the completed song. At the first showing of this version, Godard confronted Quarrier and punched him out.

p. 30   worker in song

Leonard Cohen, "Chelsea Hotel."

p. 32   Dziga Vertov Group

Several of the films of Godard's most intensely political period are signed not by him personally, but by a collective — a collaborative "group," named after the experimental Soviet film-maker Dziga Vertov, best known for *Man with a Movie Camera* (1929). In effect, the "Group" consisted mainly of Godard himself and Jean-Pierre Gorin.

p. 32   Beloved comrade Rosa/Vladimir

The sound track of *Pravda* consists of a dialogue between two voices, but the characters speaking (or rather, reading) never appear on screen.

They address each other as "Beloved comrade Vladimir" and "Beloved comrade Rosa." The most obvious references would be to Lenin, and to the German Communist leader Rosa Luxemburg (murdered in 1919). However, two years later, in the film actually called *Vladimir and Rosa*, the two characters are identified as Friedrich (as in Engels) Vladimir, and Karl (as in Marx) Rosa: the Rosa of the later film is emphatically male.

p. 37   Pig circus
Bob Dylan, "Hurricane," a song about another inglorious episode in American justice.

p. 37   Jean-Luc and Jean-Pierre
Godard and Gorin; see pages 80–81, note to page 32. Godard is an avid tennis player, and appears, actually playing, in J L G / J L G .

p. 37   know which way the wind blows
Bob Dylan, "Subterranean Homesick Blues." Dylan's line — "You don't need a weatherman to know which way the wind blows" — was, rather oddly, the source for the name of the American revolutionary group The Weathermen. Godard's soundtrack repeatedly plays an insipid rock song about the romance between a Weather Man and a Weather Girl, which, to my relief, I have been unable to trace.

p. 37   Some of us are prisoners
Bob Dylan, "George Jackson," about the Black Panther leader shot by prison guards. By sheer coincidence, I happened to hear "George Jackson," for the first time in many years, on the same day that, for the first time in many more years, I re-watched *Vladimir and Rosa*. Godard's film and Dylan's song came out in the same year, 1971.

p. 38   motorcycle crash
Dylan's much-mythologized motorcycle crash took place in 1966; Godard's, medically much more serious, in 1971.

p. 38   it's all good
This phrase, a literal translation of "Tout va bien," became a common cliché in America in the early 21st century. Its vacuity is viciously and gleefully satirized by Dylan in his 2009 song of the same name.

p. 38   big-time movie stars
Jane Fonda and Yves Montand, the lead actors in *Tout Va Bien*. Fonda is also the unwitting "star" of Godard and Gorin's polemical *Letter to Jane*.

p. 40   three dying generations
The image of three generations — children, parents, grandparents — is repeated frequently throughout Godard's later films. I have added the allusion to W.B. Yeats, "Sailing to Byzantium."

pp. 41, 45   Libération
French daily newspaper, founded by Jean-Paul Sartre, with a left-wing bias and (to me) an impenetrable prose style.

p. 42   Duras / truck
Marguerite Duras, novelist and film-maker, almost appears in *Sauve Qui Peut*. Her voice from a taped interview is heard on the soundtrack, supposedly coming from the back seat of a car — but the supposed speaker is never shown. Duras' films include *India Song* (my favourite) and *Le Camion* (The Truck).

p. 42   My landlady
Paule Muret plays a small but crucial role in this film: she is the mother in the final scene. Many years later, I internet-rented an apartment on the place Saint-Sulpice in Paris, and was amazed and delighted to discover that my landlady had appeared in a Godard film.

p. 45   bring[ing] it all back home
Title of a Bob Dylan album.

p. 46   fail[ing] to understand
Bob Dylan, "Drifter's Escape."

p. 46   that American movie
Carmen Jones (1954), directed by Otto Preminger.

p. 46   it's called the dawn
Adapted from the closing lines of Godard's film, which are in turn adapted from Jean Giraudoux, *Electra* (1937).

p.47   *Le livre de Marie*
A 30-minute film, luminous and beautiful, by Godard's partner, Anne-Marie Miéville, which is always included as a prelude to *Je Vous Salue, Marie*.

pp. 47, 48   *Absolutely … ruins of your balcony*
Bob Dylan, "Absolutely Sweet Marie."

pp. 47, 48   *contempt in the background*
In one scene of *Le Livre de Marie*, a TV set in the background is showing Godard's *Le Mépris*.

p. 47   *schedule of trains*
Leonard Cohen, "The Stranger Song."

p. 48   *Bunuel's eye*
The infamous opening shot of Luis Bunuel's *Un Chien Andalou* (1929) shows an eyeball being sliced open.

p. 49   *no direction home*
Bob Dylan, "Like a Rolling Stone."

p. 50   *"Le Prince d'Aquitaine"*
Gerard de Nerval; quoted by Eliot as one of the "fragments … shored against my ruins" in *The Waste Land*.

p. 50   *actors and stars*
Godard's credits mischievously distinguish between "actors" (Jean-Pierre Léaud, Laurent Terzieff) and "stars" (Nathalie Baye, Claude Brasseur, Alain Cuny, Johnny Hallyday).

p. 52   *Meanwhile there is music being made*
The action of *Soigne Ta Droite* is interspersed with shots of a pop music duo, Les Rita Mitsouko, developing songs in the recording studio — very similar to the footage of The Rolling Stones in *One Plus One*, in that Godard is more interested in the process than in the final product.

pp. 53, 54   I fear I am not in my perfect mind
Shakespeare, *King Lear*. The line is in fact quoted in *Soigne Ta Droite*,
anticipating Godard's next film, *King Lear*.

p. 54   blood on the tracks, desire
Dylan album titles.

p. 54   famous writer
Norman Mailer. Mailer provided a script for the film, which Godard
largely ignored. Mailer and his daughter Kate filmed one scene, which
Godard did use, before leaving the production.

p. 54   A violent silence
Godard drew this phrase from French critic Viviane Forrester, *La violence
du calme* (1980).

p. 54   O what dear daughter
Bob Dylan, "Tears of Rage."

p. 54   fragments I have shored
Eliot, *The Waste Land*

pp. 54, 62   quotations on the Wall
Bob Dylan, "Love Minus Zero / No Limit." But with a capital W, in 1987,
also the Berlin Wall.

p. 54   Le roi Lire
Bilingual pun: King Lear/the King of Reading. I remember this headline
from a French magazine reviewing Godard's film, but, though I loved
the pun, I cannot recall the exact source.

pp. 54, 63   the time of resurrection
Godard attributes the phrase "The image will appear in the time of
resurrection" to Saint Paul, but I have been unable to trace the source.
My brother Charles, Professor of New Testament Theology, assures me
that it does *not* appear in Saint Paul.

p. 55   And in me too the wave rises … Percival

Virginia Woolf, *The Waves*. The conclusion of Godard's film is an extraordinary collage of Woolf and Shakespeare. The film actually shows a paperback copy of Woolf's novel washing ashore on Lac Léman. The phrase "against death" occurs both in the closing of Woolf's novel and in Madeleine's line from *Masculin Féminin*. "Why then, she lives" is, in Shakespeare, Lear's final, exquisite delusion about Cordelia; Godard redemptively allows it to be the last line of his film.

p. 56   Every blessed line

The story goes that the film's star, Alain Delon, demanded a written script, so Godard provided him with a "written" script, every line derived from a previous author.

p. 56   Certain gardens

Ian Hamilton Finlay, "Disconnected Sentences About Gardening."

p. 59   games with … names

The French word "hélas" means "alas," but also puns on "Hellas," the Greek name for Greece. But I don't think "all Greek to me" is idiomatic in French. The publicity for this film about a god come to earth further punned bilingually on the names of its star and director: deparD I E U / G O D ard. Several of the characters bear names derived from Godard's family.

p. 59   A messenger arrives

Bob Dylan, "Changing of the Guard."

p. 60   the Kingdom of France

Shakespeare, *King Lear*.

p. 62   One doesn't trifle with love in Sarajevo

This was the original title of *For Ever Mozart*. It derives from a play by Alfred de Musset (1810–1857), *On ne badine pas avec l'amour*, which the young group of actors in the film propose to perform in Sarajevo.

p. 62   without a cause

Nicholas Ray, *Rebel Without a Cause* (1955), with James Dean.

p. 62   always answer No
Bob Dylan, "Tears of Rage."

p. 63   Debbie, let's go home
John Ford, *The Searchers* (1956). The climactic line of the film, spoken
by John Wayne to Natalie Wood, is a scene much loved by Godard, and
quoted in *Histoire(s) du Cinéma*. (In Ford's film, the line is actually "Let's
go home, Debbie," but I have inverted it for reasons of rhythm.)

p. 64   But first Elpenor came
Ezra Pound, "Canto I":

>   But first Elpenor came, our friend Elpenor,
>   Unburied, cast on the wide earth,
>   Limbs that we left in the house of Circe,
>   Unwept, unwrapped in sepulchre, since toils urged other.
>   Pitiful spirit.

This passage is quoted in full by Godard at the very end of *Histoire(s)*
du Cinéma.

p. 65   (1a)
This poem is my attempt to reproduce on the page a sequence in
Histoire(s) du Cinéma in which Godard weaves an elaborate collage of
scenes and sounds, including references to Alfred Hithcock; Henri
Langlois (founder of the Cinémathèque Française); *Man with a Movie*
Camera (Dziga Vertov: see page 80, note to page 32); the "Lie to me"
dialogue from *Johnny Guitar*; and the song "If It Be Your Will," written
and performed by Leonard Cohen.

p. 66   The Voyage of Edgar
"a 1938 adventure book by Edouard Peisson, mentioned by Johnny
Hallyday in *Detective*, that Godard had loved as a child" — Richard
Brody.

p. 67   point of no return / Oh David, tristesse
One of the characters in the final sequence of *Notre Musique* is reading
Street of No Return, by David Goodis. See also page 78, note to page 20.

p. 68   upper deck
Bob Dylan, "Senor."

p. 68   and the ship sails on
E la nave va, film by Federico Fellini (1983).

p. 69   just kids
Title of Patti Smith's memoir, 2010.

p. 70   Tarantula lighting
The photo of Simone Weil shows one side of her face in light, one in
shadow, in high contrast — lighting also used by Jerry Schatzberg in a
famous photo of Bob Dylan, which appears on the cover of Dylan's novel
Tarantula, and which is also quoted by Godard in *Masculin Féminin*.

Other Titles from The University of Alberta Press

The Measure of Paris

STEPHEN SCOBIE

356 pages | B&W photographs, index
Wayfarer Series
978-0-88864-533-3 | $29.95 (T) paper
978-0-88864-588-3 | $23.99 (T) EPUB
978-0-88864-651-4 | $23.99 (T) Amazon Kindle
Literary Nonfiction/Cultural Studies/Memoir

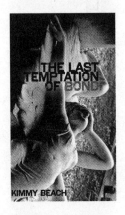

The Last Temptation of Bond

KIMMY BEACH

120 pages
Robert Kroetsch Series
978-0-88864-643-9 | $19.95 (T) paper
978-0-88864-710-8 | $15.99 (T) EPUB
978-0-88864-711-5 | $15.99 (T) Amazon Kindle
978-0-88864-808-2 | $15.99 (T) Web PDF
Poetry/Canadian Literature/Pop Culture

Massacre Street

PAUL ZITS

128 pages
Robert Kroetsch Series
978-0-88864-675-0 | $19.95 (T) paper
978-0-88864-819-8 | $15.99 (T) Web PDF
Poetry/Canadian Literature/Historiography